This book belongs to:

____

Made in the USA
Middletown, DE
06 June 2022

66768148R00070